Turn On Your Hope Light

Overcoming Chronic Illness through Faith

Lisa Kiltz

Published by

Burkhart Books

Bedford, Texas
www.BurkhartBooks.com

Dedication

*F*irst, to my Heavenly Father. Without His tender mercy, forgiveness, and desire to have my whole heart and soul, I would not be here today.

*T*o my Lord, Jesus Christ, who made a way for all to live on earth as it is in heaven. No greater love exists.

*T*o the Holy Spirit who brings comfort, guidance, and power to my days; the presence of God in me.

*T*o my Eternal Family in Christ who sacrificed, prayed, and petitioned God on my behalf for revelation knowledge, wisdom, and healing.

*T*o those who have mentored and journeyed with me along the way, being God's love and comfort in my life; God's literal shelter in the storm.

*T*o the ministries that so boldly seek God, asking Him for more of His divine mysteries, and so generously feed the sheep without fear or hesitation.

*T*o the doctors and caregivers who sacrificially risk it all, helping those in desperate need—keeping us alive while we work out our salvation. May the glorious God of heaven and earth pour out blessing upon blessing over you and assure you that your reward is waiting.

Contents

Introduction

It is my greatest joy and pleasure to be a child of the Living God! He reveals to my spirit things I could never see in the natural. As each trial and heartache encounters my inmost being, the Lord moves me through with such grace, love, and tender mercy to a position far above the place I was before. I find myself overcoming. He never fails to amaze me. Words can't describe His passion toward those who are devoted to Him. It is my prayer that you live as an Overcomer and trust in the Lord every moment of your life.

Faithful is He who calls you,
and He also will bring it to pass.

1 Thessalonians 5:24

My Story

My name is Lisa Kiltz. I am a devoted follower of Jesus Christ. To the glory of God, this is my healing testimony.

It was December of 2011; I was Christmas shopping at a mall in Salt Lake City, UT. I began to feel light-headed and dizzy, so I went to get something to eat (assuming it was low blood sugar). When I finished eating, I started to walk around and began to feel worse. I had a strong urge to sit down and need for water, so I went into one of the stores and asked to have a seat as the room began to spin. I remember pleading with one of the store employees to allow me to lie down but was unable to because of store policy. It was then an off duty EMT, who had been shopping in the store, saw and stayed with me until an ambulance arrived. I was then examined and released to go home and rest.

Do not forget to entertain strangers, for by so doing some have unwittingly entertained angels.

Hebrews 13:2

For the next two months, I began to experience a substantial increase in dizziness, vision problems, and memory loss. I was in and out of doctors' offices and hospitals only to have "negative" and "unremarkable" results on medical tests and scans. By the third month, severe drops in blood pressure, tachycardia (irregular heartbeat), and chest pain were almost unbearable. The emergency room was beginning to be a weekend activity. While having these episodes, additional medical imaging revealed a large congenital defect (hole) in my heart. This discovery was believed to be an explanation for the multitude of health issues, but the surgery provided only momentary hope as I continued to decline.

My flesh and my heart fail:
but God is the strength of my heart,
and my portion forever.

Psalm 73:26

From the time symptoms began in 2011, I was covered with healing prayer. Faithful brothers and sisters in the Lord sacrificially gave of themselves week after week. Unfortunately, symptoms began to worsen and more were added. Day and night I prayed, believed,

and stood on God's promises of healing. Prayer rooms and the testimonies of others who had been healed by the Lord consumed my time. However, three things were very clear: 1) for some reason I was still alive 2) I still had no diagnosis, and 3) there was absolutely no progress. I knew it was time to seek the Lord on a whole new level and place ALL of my trust in Him as He made a way.

⟲⟳

If any of you lacks wisdom, let him ask of God,
who gives to all liberally and without reproach,
and it will be given to him.

James 1:5

⟲⟳

In the summer of 2012, shortly after the hole in my heart was closed with the medical device, I was able to meet with a pastor for counsel and strategic prayer. I knew I was declining extremely fast, so we asked the Lord to open a door QUICKLY as there was clearly a time-sensitive issue at hand. The pastor also encouraged me to seek the Lord with certain questions that helped me discern if it was truly God's will for me to leave the mission field where I had been serving for five years? As we prayed, we completely believed that God would answer and open a door that I could walk through by faith, knowing it was His will. The door opened within three days!

⟨⟩⟩⟩⟨⟨

*I know your works. See, I have set before you an
open door, and no one can shut it;
for you have a little strength, have kept
My word and have not denied My name.*

Revelation 3:8

⟨⟩⟩⟩⟨⟨

I had received a call from a ministry in west Texas
that had been given my name through another ministry
in the Fort Worth area. They asked if I would be interested
in coming to work with them. I explained that I was still
in the process of recovering from heart surgery (knowing
I was still declining). However, I agreed to go and meet
with them. I knew that contact was the "open door" God
had placed before me.

❦

Behold, I will do a new thing,
now it shall spring forth;
Shall you not know it?
I will even make a road in the wilderness
And rivers in the desert.

Isaiah 43:19

❦

Leaving all of my belongings behind, I made my way from Utah to Texas late September 2012. The symptoms were increasing and almost unbearable. It took me three long days to get back. By the time I settled at my mother's house, I knew I was not going to be able to take any job or attempt to journey any further. There was also a very clear realization in my spirit that I was now declining at a VERY rapid rate. So much so, that I wrote my funeral arrangements and obituary on October 25, 2012.

❦

*I call heaven and earth as witnesses today against
you, that I have set before you life and death,
blessing and cursing; therefore choose life,
that both you and your descendants may live.*

Deuteronomy 30:19

❦

Although this realization was clear, I felt a strong urgency by the Holy Spirit to go and meet with the ministry in west Texas. I had not connected with a church since I arrived because of my physical limitations. By then, standing and breathing were a huge challenge. Episodes of dizziness were to the point of not being able to see clearly or be oriented with my surroundings. Flu-like symptoms and pain were ever increasing. Needless to say, I spent most of the time laying down, praying, and calling on the Name of Jesus. Although I was suffering tremendously, God graced me with enough strength to make my way to west Texas. It was there I was able to spend three days with precious women of God who prayed for and encouraged me. However, it was on the second day when I met a particular Christian woman, that God totally changed the course of my healing journey and life.

❧

*Now may the God of hope fill you with all joy and
peace in believing, that you may abound in hope
by the power of the Holy Spirit.*

Romans 15:13

❧

The last day I was there, I got a call informing me that the woman I had met was going to send me to a doctor in Fort Worth. He was a toxicologist and a master diagnostician, but did not take insurance. I was then told she would pay for EVERYTHING! Tears of hope streamed down my face as I cried out in praise and thanksgiving to the LORD. Only He could give such mercy and love. Finally, I would have an answer! God was so gracious in teaching me so much about His provision with each step of the healing journey. Over the course of the next year, this woman mailed me $3,000 a month for any medical care I needed! I truly believe this was God's provision and mercy to keep me alive as I gained more and more wisdom and revelation of His ways.

⟨~~~⟩

Trust in the LORD with all your heart,
And lean not on your own understanding;
In all your ways acknowledge Him,
And He shall direct your paths.

Proverbs 3:5-6

⟨~~~⟩

When I made it back to Fort Worth I called to make an appointment with the doctor. Although he had a long wait list for new patients, miraculously there was a break in his schedule and I was seen within two weeks. On the day of the appointment he spent several hours with me, and within two weeks we knew what was plaguing me—Babesia duncai (a co-infection of Lyme Disease). I began taking antibiotics and anti-parasitic medication, but by then it was too late. The next month I went into liver failure, placing me in the hospital for three weeks where the debilitating, aggressive symptoms continued to torment. All I had was Jesus! Faithful brothers and sisters in the Lord were still praying as doctors suggested a liver transplant. I cried out to my Healer and Great Physician. Miraculously, after the third week, my liver began healing—Praise God! I was then released from the hospital after receiving extensive treatment. Although the doctors assured me this would be all the treatment

I would need, within two weeks, IT was back with a vengeance!

⟨≈≈≈⟩

*For I, the LORD your God will hold your right
hand, Saying to you, "Fear not, I will help you."*

Isaiah 41:13

⟨≈≈≈⟩

The one thing I knew by then is that there wasn't enough money or medicine in the world to cure this destructive disease. I kept asking the Lord to reveal to me deeper revelation. He began to place people in my life one at a time who had experienced the same devastation. Each person had pursued various treatments in a variety of ways. Even I kept seeking doctors and alternative healthcare practitioners while I continued to walk through "the valley of the shadow of death …" (Psalm 23:4). I just knew in my spirit that it had to be the Lord who would deliver me from this since I had never heard of anyone who had been fully healed of this devastating disease. Until one day …

❧

God is our refuge and strength,
A very present help in trouble.

Psalm 46:1

❧

As I continued to seek the LORD, I saw an old friend at a healing ministry conference. She shared with me that her husband had been healed of Lyme disease and that I should talk to him. She arranged for me to meet with him one afternoon. He sat me down at their kitchen table and very seriously asked me, "Do you believe this could be a spiritual issue?" I said, "Absolutely." You see, my question to the Lord had not been WHY did I get sick, but HOW?

Since becoming ill, I had been receiving healing prayer several times a week, believing God for healing and standing on His Promises. During one of those times, the Lord spoke to the one praying that there was something more He wanted to reveal to me—a place of revelation and understanding I had not known before. If the Lord wanted to answer my HOW, then I was more than ready to listen.

⁕

And you will seek Me and find Me,
when you search for Me with all your heart.

Jeremiah 29:13

⁕

My friend's husband began to share with me his testimony and how he had been through a ministry that dealt with how people get sick. He strongly encouraged me to go through as well. And by the grace of God, I was able to attend immediately. When I arrived, I was still VERY sick and could barely stand or breathe. I still had flu-like symptoms with dizziness and had lost most of the color in my face. Pain and memory loss were ever present—pure torment! I drug myself into the conference, sat on the floor in a corner while listening to the words of the enemy saying, "this will never work" and "you've heard all of this before." You see, I was a huge believer in the healing power of God and saw it firsthand in the lives of others. I knew I was at a crossroad because six months after my initial symptoms I started to lose hope and give up. My physical body just became too much for me to bear. I was done. During those dark days, I remember the prayers of the faithful who had overcome their own battles praying for me. I truly believe that is what gave me the strength to make

it to that point. Now, all my chips were in and I was betting the farm on GOD!

⟳~~~⟲

Be sober, be vigilant; because your adversary the devil walks about like a roaring lion, seeking whom he may devour.

1 Peter 5:8

⟳~~~⟲

There I sat, in the corner on the floor, convinced by the enemy I was wasting my time when the teaching of the Word of God began. My ears began to hear in a new way. A veil began to lift from me and I began to see clearer. I kept overhearing the volunteers and others share their healing testimonies and how they overcame sickness and disease. I observed and listened. It wasn't until the end of the second day that things began to change for me. For the first time in 2 years, I felt my immune system slightly reboot. Meaning, when a healthy person begins to recover from sickness, it happens in a few days. I had been on a steady, volatile decline and could not remember what good health felt like. What was different on that day? I had the revelation that "a broken heart dries up the bones." (Proverbs 17:22) You see, the bones carry the immune system and cellular response to fight disease.

So, when the heart is broken by anyone or anything in life, ONLY the perfect love of our Heavenly Father can cure it. THIS IS WHERE MY HEALING BEGAN—when I received the unconditional love and acceptance of my Heavenly Father. This was not in the way I did when I received my salvation through Jesus Christ, but in the way of knowing Him as Abba Father. It began an intimate relationship of me as a child putting all affection, confidence, and trust into my loving Daddy. My heart began to heal and feel so much love in a way I had never felt before. I knew this was the path I was to follow … and doors continued to open.

For I am persuaded that neither death nor life,
nor angels nor principalities nor powers,
nor things present nor things to come, nor height
nor depth, nor any other created thing,
shall be able to separate us from the love of God
which is in Christ Jesus our Lord.

Romans 8:38-39

It was after that day that I spent the next few years discovering what I know now as finding out who God created me to be from the foundation of the world

(Jeremiah 1:5) … and continue to do so. You see, when we are born, we are "perfectly and wonderfully made" (Psalm 139:14). Then, we enter into a place unbeknownst to us (earth). From that point on, we begin to be "conformed to the image of this world" (Romans 12:2) and are shaped by the people and happenings all around us. That is, until we surrender our life to God, our Creator. We come to know him by the grace of His Holy Spirit, drawing us to Himself (John 6:44). God the Father literally purchased your life and mine with the blood sacrifice of His One and Only Son, Jesus Christ (Galatians 3:13). By doing this, He made it possible to be reconciled to Him; to live now and eternally with Him forever. In this covenant relationship, we have the privilege of hearing His Voice and having His leading and guidance (John 10:27). He also gives wisdom and revelation knowledge (Ephesians 1:17) to those who seek Him with their whole heart (Jeremiah 29:13). For this to happen, you must be born again (John 3:3) and receive His Holy Spirit (Acts 19:2). This is God's desire for all of mankind.

⟶≈≈⟵

*And they overcame him by the blood of the Lamb
and by the word of their testimony,
and they did not love their lives to the death.*

Revelation 12:11

⟶≈≈⟵

I'd like to say it was a steady climb to healing by overcoming, but it was also a battle. And this battle is not for the faint of heart. I can remember the saints that would pray for "my spirit to rise up and fight" when my body and soul were left for dead. You see, when you go through the surrender of the physical body, you MUST rely on His strength (2 Corinthians 12:9) and be completely confident He will give you what you need when you need it. It can be a very dark place, and only His light can penetrate it (John 1:5). We must look to find Him deep within us. You can rest easy in this—God holds the key to each person's heart and knows the way He will take them. You DO NOT want to miss what He is trying to accomplish in your soul (3 John 1:2). This is far greater than focusing on the physical healing. We learn to do this by adjusting our whole self to HEARING, TRUSTING, and OBEYING Him every moment of our lives.

᠆᠆᠆᠆

And we know that all things work together for
good to those who love God,
to those who are called according to His purpose.

Romans 8:28

᠆᠆᠆᠆

In the fifth year of overcoming sickness and disease, I married and moved to California. Sadly, the marriage only lasted a little over a year. I will share only a few details as it relates to the broken and lonely places, but I do want to proclaim where I saw God's Mighty Hand at work during that time ...

One month after I was married, I met a cardiologist for an annual checkup. Since my heart surgery in 2012, I had been having some residual symptoms that no other doctor would address. Although I was improving, I had lived with these symptoms for quite some time. I knew I had hit a plateau with my physical healing and was unable to get a breakthrough. But this particular cardiologist said he wanted to "get to the bottom of this." So, he ordered some imaging and found the device was incorrectly placed near my mitral valve and had a defective wire sticking out. Within months the device was removed by open heart surgery—Praise God!

I remember the day my cardiologist said to me that he truly believed that God brought me to California for him to fix my heart so I could live! When he said it, my spirit had a witness that it was true. I tell you this to say that we cannot place limits on God. Our only task is to learn how to HEAR, TRUST, and OBEY Him.

I know some of you will disagree that God would allow someone to get married in order to enter into another level of physical healing, but it happened. Honestly, I don't believe it is God's will for a marriage to end either. But, we can only do what God has given us to do and are not responsible for anyone else. I hoped and prayed that my spouse would have become a the man and husband God had destined him to be, but it just never happened. I did everything I could possibly do and reached out for help to our community of believers. We all experienced withdrawal from him.

In the middle of a very long and difficult recovery from the surgery, I sadly suffered a miscarriage. After that, I was to face another battle and heartbreak as I heard my husband tell me he made a mistake getting married, enter into fits of rage, and walk away from responsibility. Once again, I had to look to Heavenly Father's love to mend my broken heart and run into the arms of my loving Savior. I had to continually place my trust in Him, remembering He is truly "perfect in all His ways" (Psalm 18:30). The choice was set before me AGAIN to HEAR, TRUST, and OBEY Him. What I found to be true in the midst of a very difficult time is that God is more interested in delivering

those who are fully devoted to Him than leaving them to die a slow spiritual death in situations that bring no glory to Him.

❦

But may the God of all grace,
who called us to His eternal glory by Christ Jesus,
after you have suffered a while,
perfect, establish, strengthen, and settle you.

1 Peter 5:10

❦

It wasn't until the seventh year that my body recovered. The number seven in the Bible represents completion and perfection. There is something about the number seven! Isn't that just like God? His timing for each one of us is perfect, and one thing is FOR SURE—the completed work Jesus Christ did for us on the cross allows and enables us to receive salvation from sin and death, be healed in our soul and body, and be delivered from our enemy. It is critical for us to settle this in our hearts. It is our inheritance as sons and daughters of the Most High God (Psalm 103:1-5). This belief is vital to how we walk out our Christian life and learn to overcome. We should never minimize this or take it for granted. Jesus made the ultimate sacrifice and paid the

highest price on our behalf. To deny or doubt this is to deny and doubt His very purpose and Person. We must resist forming our own belief system based on our five senses (what we see, hear, taste, smell, and touch), what we experience, and our human reason. In that realm, there is no faith involved. We must believe that "God is not a liar" (Numbers 23:19) and that He does what He says and says what He does. This will lift the Spirit of Fear (2 Timothy 1:7) from you, then faith can abound; and this pleases God (Hebrews 11:6).

❦

Satan has asked to sift all of you as wheat.
But I have prayed for you, that your faith
may not fail. And when you have turned back,
strengthen your brothers.

Luke 22:31-32

❦

From start to finish, I had received a diagnosis of environmental illness due to black mold exposure, Lyme disease and co-infections, liver failure, heart failure, Transient Ischemic Attacks, a large defect (hole) in my heart, 30-40% memory loss and the ability to process information, post-traumatic pericarditis from the trauma of heart surgery (which is excruciatingly painful

by the way), and a miscarriage. I have also experienced a few things through my teenage years and twenties that I left out. Combine this with rejection, abandonment, and the soul damage from personal experiences, it was so diabolical that ONLY the Lord could restore, deliver, and heal me.

I know there will always be skeptics, those who doubt and those who will live their entire life by personal experience and look no further. Some may even ask, "Couldn't the Lord have healed you in a moment?" The answer is, "Yes." Did He? No, although I did have some miraculous healings along the way as I learned to listen to what He desired of me. Why? I believe we all have a unique purpose and destiny to fulfill that brings glory to God in a unique and specific way. The calling and gifts He gives are indeed irrevocable (Romans 11:29) and make room for us (Proverbs 18:16). So, we must be changed. We must be broken. And He will not relent until He has our whole heart.

Most of the time, the healing journey is very lonely. We often feel like giving up, but don't! It is just something we must accept. It will never look like what we think it should. At times, friends and family are lost and often replaced by others who will walk with us. But most people will never fully understand. To expect more will always bring disappointment, but there is One who will never let us down (Romans 5:5). He is the wonderful Presence and Person of Jesus Christ found in His Holy Spirit. He is the ONLY One we can rely on. He is Faithful

and True (Revelation 19:11). He will NEVER leave or forsake us (Hebrews 13:5). And that, my friend, will ALWAYS BE ENOUGH.

Today I write to you knowing I am still on my healing journey of overcoming. In October 2018, I learned that I had developed a "predominant" cyst on the right pericardium of my heart from the trauma of surgery. Over the next couple of months, the Lord put it in my spirit to go to a healing and prophesy ministry retreat over New Year's Eve. After several days of going deeper into the presence of God and receiving much prayer and ministry, I was filled with peace. I left with no fear and was looking forward to seeing how the Lord would lead and guide me as I learned, EVEN MORE, to HEAR, TRUST, and OBEY Him. Six months later, my follow up CT scan revealed there was little to no cyst left, but a "redistribution of fluid." Praise God! However, prior to my follow-up scan I had developed a severe case of pericarditis. By God's grace, through my precious brothers and sisters in Christ, I was able to travel to California to see my cardiologist without any expense. There, I was able to have more imaging and tests. After my evaluation, the cardiologist felt my heart was functioning fine and did not believe there was anything to be concerned with. Praise God!

It was also during the time in California I realized how much closure and healing I still needed from the past—another type of heart healing. I've come to realize that sometimes physical things are very symbolic of what

is happening spiritually or emotionally. It was there the Lord healed the heartbreak of a shattered dream. It was a place of deep forgiveness, gratitude, grief, and acceptance. It was there that a glimmer of hope for the future birthed again.

You see, God holds the key to each one of our hearts and will speak differently to each person. What I want you to know is that all things really are possible when you seek Him with your whole heart. He cares about every detail of your life and loves you with an everlasting love!

I encourage everyone who reads this to share your own testimony. Don't be afraid to look at what the Lord is doing deep inside as well as out. WRITE IT DOWN and GET IT OUT THERE for the entire world to hear! The Lord revealed to me that it is the seed that will scatter to future generations and is our legacy—His legacy! It is our living testimony. Just as those who were led by the Holy Spirit to write the inspired Scriptures, we too are responsible for sharing the goodness and faithfulness of the One, True, Living God (Jeremiah 10:10-13)! To Him be the glory and honor forever and ever! Amen.

To Be Continued!

Final Thoughts

I don't go into a lot of the intimate details of what God revealed to me personally because God will speak differently to each person. I can tell you that there was instant, miraculous healing in my lungs when the Lord spoke to me to go to a church and have a particular person pray for me. There were quiet times when the Lord told me to repent, which brought a degree of healing. There were times He revealed to me to break off generational curses and spirits that were afflicting me. I felt the presence of angels and saw demons—confirming it was indeed a spiritual battle; and so much more! What the Lord has shown me recently is that our terminology has gotten confused. People talk all the time of seeking their healing when pursuing the things of natural man. I believe God uses natural man; however, I believe what they really mean is they are looking for a CURE. A cure comes from the outside in, while true health and healing come from the inside out (3 John 1:2). I really believe that the healing journey is OVERCOMING (Revelation 12:11). And, in Christ, we overcome the world, our flesh, and the enemy! The ministry resources I have provided in this book will give you the tools of understanding to receive your own revelation of overcoming. He cares

about every detail of your life and loves you with an everlasting love! God bless and keep you. I will be praying for you, that your spirit would rise up and fight. And, that you overcome by the blood of the Lamb and the word of your testimony. Amen!

Special Recognition

Be in Health™ Ministries, Thomaston, GA
Dr. Sarkis Baghdasarian, Fresno, CA
Dr. Charles Hamel & Staff, Arlington, TX
Dr. Gerald Harris, Fort Worth, TX
Dr. Hon Lee, Santa Clara, CA
Aquilla Nash Ministries, Longview, TX
Pathway to Heath Ministries, Orlando, FL
Dr. Ron Wilson & Staff, Denton, TX
Andrew Wommack Ministries International™

About the Author

Lisa Kiltz is a follower of her First Love, Jesus Christ, who has forgiven, healed, and set her free. Her passion is to see individual's be made whole (body, soul and spirit) while walking out their God-given destiny. She surrendered her life to Jesus Christ in 1998 and has served in missions and with a variety of ministries and organizations. Her background includes a Master of Arts in Christian Ministry, Bachelor of Science & Biology, Clinical Pastoral Education, Social Services, and Clinical Care.

Her life verse is Romans 8:28,

And we know [with great confidence]
that God [who deeply loves and cares for us]
causes all things to work together for the good
of those who love Him, who are called according
to His purpose.

lisakiltz.blogspot.com

lisakiltzbooks@gmail.com

Made in the USA
Coppell, TX
22 November 2019